# How to Justify Your Price: Identity Unique Benefits That Increase Value

Category: Business & Economics

Author: Bob Oros

Publisher: Bob Oros Publishing

ISBN: 978-1-387-19915-0

Copyright 2017

Description: If you don't know the reasons that justify your price, it is important to find out what those reasons are. When your price is higher because you have added too much profit you will never make the sale. When you justify your price because you added value, you will make the sale.

Key words: wholesale sales training, distributor sales training, food service sales, sales coaching, sales techniques, motivating sales people, job in sales, sales manager training, sales course, manufacturing sales training, online sales training, food sales jobs,

ISBN 978-1-387-19915-0

## 1. How can you justify rather than discount?

If you don't know the reasons that justify your price, it is important to find out what those reasons are.

The business department of a major university conducted a test on 100 companies. They divided them into three groups according to how they sold.

The first group of 30 companies sold strictly on price. The sales people had as much flexibility as they felt they needed to get the business.

The second group of 40 companies was allowed to give heavily controlled price discounts.

The third group of 30 companies gave no discounts and sold at book price.

The results...

Group one sold the least amount on a per sales person basis, earned less gross profit, return on investment was the poorest in the industry. Price buyers would search for the sales people who sell on price and try to squeeze the price even lower. The sales people constantly complained that there was no loyalty among buyers.

Group two had a higher sales per person than group one, earned a higher gross profit and had a better return on investment. The sales people complained that if they had lower prices they could sell more.

Group three had the highest per person sales, the highest gross profit and the best return on investment. THE SALES PEOPLE WERE BETTER TRAINED IN SELLING STRATEGIES AND WERE ABLE JUSTIFY THEIR PRICE RATHER THAN DISCOUNT IT!

Here are some of the things a sales person might say to justify the price:

"Yes, our price is higher - but our product has longer shelf life.  You will never lose any money because of spoilage. We get it in and out of our warehouse and onto your shelf faster than any other distributor."

Then show them the comparative figures on spoilage. Highlight this benefit they cannot get anywhere else.

Or you might say:  "Yes, our machine costs $30 more-but other machines can cost you twice that $30 saving every few months in repairs.   Here are the frequency of repair records for our machine and for our two top competitors. "Show him the figures-and then make your big point.  'A machine that hardly ever needs service and repairs is a tremendous advantage today, when service is so expensive and hard to come by. "

Here are some reasons your buyers will pay more for.

When your customer trusts and knows what to expect from you, you gain an advantage. Consistent quality, delivery, service, and constant innovation create exceptional value in a sale.

When you can demonstrate that your products are guaranteed to arrive in perfect condition, you increase your value.

When a customer perceives that your company responds instantly to their problem, the customer will do business with you again.

Your product may cost less for operator training, a lower cost to run, and reduced cost to repair than a competitive offering.

Customers will select a technically sound company over one that's obsolete or on the brink of failure.

Your customer will pay more to eliminate and avoid headaches.

--------------------------------

Comments:

--------------------------------

Often times, some of our customers don't want to hear the reasons our products cost more. Many times, their customers wish they would.

**Jim Ruth**


People do not buy on low price - they buy on value. Sometimes that is the lowest price but that is rare. A good salesperson constantly hones their skills to promote the value of their product and services just as a buyer continuously works on their skills to determine the best value for their dollar.

When the customer believes that your price is higher because you have added too much profit you will never sell them. When they believe your price is higher because you have spent money to increase the value of your product/service you will usually make the sale.

The "new guy" in business usually jumps at the lowball offer but, with experience, learns that it will lower his profits in the long run.

**Crocker Smith**

You must be able to justify qualities and benefits of your product/service to reinforce your price. If I am giving 100% of my time, energy, and life why would I consider discounting my price? My service and quality are not "discounted" so why should my price be? Bob sums this up in one important sentence.........

"When your customer trusts and knows what to expect from you, you gain an advantage. Consistent quality, delivery, service, and constant innovation create exceptional value in a sale."

**Brooke Knight**


We must be fully informed of all of our services and be prepared for any type of question they may throw at us. If they ask us a question and we get stumped, how does that make us look? We have to be informed of not only our services and what we offer, but also on our potential clients

company. Do research on them before you ever walk in their door.

**Kimberly Burgess**

I'd much rather have to explain the reason(s) for a higher price than have to apologize to the customer for unacceptable quality.

**Doug Barringer**


It's important to inform your customer why the prices are what they are. Sometimes it's supply and demand, bad weather or a number of other reasons. What ever the reason you shouldn't make something up always get the facts.

**Scott Forgie**


I am currently focusing more on service, rather than just selling cases. I deliver twice or more a week and will haul product in my car to correct mistakes, either the customers or my own. I answer the phone on weekends. I answer the phone at night. I respond to customer requests for new products, better products or service issues as rapidly as possible. I look for value added items to upgrade and save them labor or cut their waste.

I deserve to be paid and I deserve job security. If I can't make a living, if my company can't make a profit delivering my accounts, what's the point? I am beginning to communicate this to my customers more often. I am WORTH a little more. They aren't paying for higher priced groceries, they are paying for ME and the exceptional service and quality my company offers.

**Chris Chase**


Well the best way to justify rather than discount is to know exactly what your company can do for the potential customer, and then know exactly what services you can offer as well. By doing this you can grab the attention with other features rather than price. If you can show that you can offer the customer a lot more than just a price then price will not matter.

**Jason Kirouac**

## 2. What do people base their decisions on?

Have you ever laughed at a joke because everybody else laughed so you felt the obligation to laugh? Have you ever bought something based on the fact that it was the "best selling" or "fastest moving" item? Would the statement "4 out of 5 people surveyed recommend this product" influence your decision? How about "over two million copies sold" on the cover of a book? Would that make you feel more comfortable about your decision to buy it? If so, you are not alone. People are highly influenced and persuaded by what others do.

I am the first customer to go through the car wash, yet the tip jar has 10 one-dollar bills folded in the jar. I am the first one in the bar and notice the bartenders tip jar already has several dollar bills in it..

Nightclub owners create long lines to give the impression that business is great. Krispy Crème Donuts has a bunch of folks camp out the night before the store opening so they can have the first donuts that are cooked – creating the impression that these donuts must be really good.

What does all this mean? It means that this concept works and it can work for you too. Here's how.

Everybody likes to think of himself or herself as a nonconformist – someone who does their own thing. You and I like to see ourselves as independent – until it comes time to make a decision – then we find out what everybody else is doing and what everybody else thinks – and conclude that they must be right – and make the decision that I am going to do the same thing.

Let's say you are a new sales person calling on a potential account. Would you say; 'I am new and don't have any customers yet – will you take a chance and be the first?"

If you were a seasoned sales person would you go into a potential customer and say; "We have great quality and excellent service?" No, you wouldn't want to say something like that because their response would be "so what." You would want to take the approach that the bartender, car wash, church, evangelical preacher and concert promoter took. You want to bring on your success stories, testimonials, references, people your prospect knows and a list of happy customers who are buying from you. You would want to put a little money in your tip jar to show that others are buying and they are happy. Why? To make them feel safe about their decision to buy from you.

---------------------------------

Comments:

---------------------------------

I made several calls on a local doctor and explained and promoted our payroll service to him. He was very skeptical at first but after the fourth call he was on board and excited about it – he could see the advantages for his practice and his employees.

He said to come by the following Monday and we would take care of all of the documents but on that Monday morning his office manager called and said that they had discussed it further and decided against it at this time. She had a defensive attitude and did not want to listen to anything I had to say.

At this point I was very tempted to "raise the level" of my tone to her but I bit my tongue and resisted. I just said '"please feel free to call me if I can help at any time". Yesterday the doctor called me and said he was ready to do the deal. His accountant had told him that this was a good thing for him to do and it would save him money (the exact same thing I had been telling him). Sometimes it takes a third party to convince a customer. I signed him up two hours later and I was able to feel comfortable around the office manager also.

But I came very close to "burning the bridge". It turns out that the office manager was also his daughter.

**Crocker Smith**


I've never been one to follow crowds, never bought the most popular car model, etc.  It seems to be a great marketing strategy though because a lot of people follow the crowds.  I remember a guy telling me one time that McDonald's had the best hamburgers.  "They had to be the best because they sold the most."  I replied telling him no they do great research on where to locate their restaurants and have a great marketing campaign.  It's funny how some people equate the most with best.

**Cary McAfee**


One of my early careers was a waiter with a chain restaurant. I wanted to move on to very upscale white table cloth restaurant in the heart of downtown where the tips would be much better. I took all my 324 comment cards, good and bad, and give them to the owner with the statement: "I would like to be a part of your team,  (he was

16

a ex-pro basketball player) and here is the best references I can give you. Most of them are outstanding, A few may not seem that good, but it's a honest review of my work." Yes I got the job and it opened up a whole new world for me.

**David Vize**


People base a lot of their decisions on what other people are doing. It seems to make more sense to use a product/service that someone you know is using and happy with, right? Not always. My personal belief is that price is not the ultimate factor. I believe it is the ability to persuade the customer into buying "ME." Of course the successful stories, references, and the list of companies we serve are just the "icing" on the cake. Then you tell your prospect, "You get "ME" and look who else has made this decision and its working perfectly!"

**Brooke Knight**


I try to be the type of person that makes up my mind based on the facts not the, "I'm doing it because every one else is doing it type." Although I have been a bartender for many years and every time I walk behind the bar I take $20.00 in ones and put them in the jar. It does work. People want to follow the crowd. If they see a bunch of ones in the jar they believe that he must be a really good bartender and stand in line waiting on me instead of getting a drink right away form a bartender with only a few dollars in there jar.

### Brian Spraggins

I like this strategy, although I must say that quoting a client's competition has come back to bite me as well. People do like to follow the crowds sometimes so letting a prospect know where and who your program is working with seems to build more credibility. It's funny thing to watch a crowd (and I have been guilty of this), migrating a certain way or waiting in a line just because it is drawing the masses.

### Kristan Wilson

We see this all the time (tip jars full, etc.) and it tends to work in most situations. Of course, when you're doing marketing and sales, you can't really carrying around a tip jar full of ones. But you can have an arsenal of success stories, situations that best represent your services. We can all do this!

### Suzanne Davis

## 3. How can you have control over the interview?

How would you like to walk into a customer's office and have a powerful tool that will give you complete control over the conversation?

You can do it. Here's how. Before you go in to see the customer carefully list five things you want to discuss. When you are in the customers office place this list where the buyer can easily see it. Without saying a word you have just taken control.

Every buyer or customer works from a list. When you place this list in front of them they will have an IRRESISTIBLE urge to work the list and check each item off. If you don't think the buyer will give you the amount of time to cover every thing you want to talk about you can solve that problem by simply using a yellow pad and a black marker.

I discovered this by accident when I was going to call on a important account and did not have the time to prepare in advance. I took out a yellow pad and made a list of five things I wanted to talk about. When I sat down in the buyers office I set the pad on the desk where the buyer could see it. I then started talking about point number one on my list.

The conversation started to get side tracked when the buyer was interrupted by a phone call. He hung up the phone, his eyes went to my list and he started talking about point number two.

His secretary entered the room and asked him to step out for a minute. When he returned his eyes again went to the list and we began discussing point number three and then four and five.

The amazing part about this is that he never became impatient with our meeting. He seemed to know that when we completed the five points I had listed on the yellow pad were all discussed we would be finished with our meeting. There were even other sales people waiting to see him and we went over my appointment time by 25 minutes.

Try it and you will be surprised at how smoothly the sales call will go.

----------------------------

Comments:

----------------------------

Being a navy recruiter we used this a lot. Based on the applicants quails we would use this in the form of brochures especially when talking to the parents. The parents would start with the top one and work thru the pile until they had them all on their side of the table including the permission form they had to sign for their child to go take the physical and join the service

**Ralph Scalici**


This definitely makes sense. This tool keeps the conversation on track especially for announced interruptions. I know anytime you go to a conference or workshop they use a handout or overhead projector. This here is the same principle. I know from my past management training classes they always said, "The key to any corporation or company recruiting new management was to pick an individual that follows directions." Obviously, sales management would also follow in that category. People have not a clue their being controlled because of the way it's been done tactfully without being agressive.

**Shawn Hollis**


That sounds like a great idea to me. I find that the first cold call with a busy person is more influenced by the prospect not knowing how long the meeting will take than what the content is. "When will this guy stop talking and let me get back to my important work?". If I find a customer is in this mode I tend to speed up my presentation to keep their interest which is not as effective. I will definitely try this.

**Crocker Smith**

In a former position we were trained to complete a call/ visit work sheet prior to our visit. On the work sheet we had our VBR (valid business reason) with a primary and secondary goal. It was a great tool to move the buying process forward. Although, I don't fill out a work sheet in my current position, I always go into a client with my Valid Business Reason and my primary goal already pre determined.

**Becky Akins**

Before I walk into any account I would always get an idea in my head of what I was going to discuss. 90% of the time I never made it past the first topic. At least I am on the right track. Now I will try writing things down on my note pad and using it to my advantage. I can see how this would help take a lot of the pressure off of both the customer and the salesman.

Here is something I was taught in Marine Corps. They called it the 6 P's.

"Proper Planning Prevents Piss Poor Performance"

**Jason Kirouac**

## 4. Why should you be impressed rather than try to impress?

How would you like to have everyone you meet be super impressed with you?  How would you like to have your customers tell everyone they know that you are the smartest sales person they have ever dealt with?

I am going to show you how and if you try it you will be amazed at the results.  You don't have to wait until your next sales call - you can try it right now.

Go and tell your spouse, partner, coworker, neighbor, or the next person you see, that you are impressed with something they are doing.

If there is nothing obvious to be impressed about look for something.  Be sincere about it.  Watch their reaction. They will think you are the smartest person they know. Why? Because you are smart enough to be impressed with something they are doing.

Now try it on one of your customers.  Once your customer knows that he or she sincerely impresses you, they will know you are one of the smartest sales people that ever called on them.

The first law of selling to another business is to realize that there are no such things as companies, only people.  You don't sell your products to some inanimate organization that makes rational decisions based on logical data. You sell to a human, emotional, somewhat irrational person who makes the decision based on issues of ego, personality and irrationality.

With this in mind you have to use the same basic principle you use to win anyone over to your way of thinking. The person you are selling to has to like you. They must believe that you know what you are talking about before they will listen to anything you have to say.

The best way to impress your customer is to let them know, in a sincere way, that you think he or she is really something. Tell them what great work they do or what an interesting business they have.

Find something you have in common. People like people who are like them. And people believe and trust people they like.

Try to discover attitudes, likes, dislikes, family backgrounds, experiences, personality virtues or quirks, careers, goals, or values that you have in common with your customers; then emphasize them.

People reason that if you're like them in some ways, you're probably like them in other ways.  Therefore, they begin to transfer trust as friend to friend.

And they will buy from you.

-------------------------------------

Comments:

-------------------------------------


I actually tried this tactic on Jenn here in the office right after I read it and sure enough it really works! I will be using this a lot more.

**Tessa Matthews**


All things in moderation; the key is sincerity and having an understanding of the subject! I have 3 Words that will help you with this: Research, Research and you got it more Research. You need to know the Company, their Product (or service) and the Decision Maker you are talking with. You are NOT going to spout information to the client. Your goal is to find content to complement your client on!!!!! NOTE: a great place to find information if the company is publicly traded is in their annual reports. This will list the company's vision, notes from the CEO, history and where they are looking to take the Company. They will be impressed in two ways. The 1st is you recognized how wonderful and smart THEY are and you did your homework.

Use it!

**Teresa Cloninger**


In my position with our company, I work with restaurant owners. I let the customer know right away I owned 3 restaurants of my own. I get 'excited' when I notice what my customers are doing "right". No one tells a restaurant owner they are doing a great job. Customers will not tell a restaurant owner that the restaurant is exceptionally clean or decorated. They come to expect perfection.

We are in the business of details. It is these details that I note and tell the customer within minutes of our meeting. I do this with every visit. I notice right away the customers focus, from exceptionally clean restaurant, great menus to signage. If I notice the outside of the restaurant neat, clean and organized, I might even point this out during our handshake.

It is noticing and noting these details that's puts the customer at ease ....to say nothing about his/her ego...

**Roland DeGregorio**

# 5. Why should you ask for advice?

How would you like to have a magic formula that would turn the toughest customer into a best friend? The next time you are faced with a really tough customer, one that always gives you a hard time about everything, try this: Ask for their advice on something.

Sound too simple? Try it and watch what happens. Ask them how they would handle a certain situation. For example, ask a customer how they would sell to a certain individual that you both know.

Ask your spouse how they would handle something. Ask a friend or neighbor how to fix something. When you say to someone "I would like to ask your advice," you can almost see the person's interest level increase.

The important point to remember when asking for advice is that it must be sincere. The best way to do that is to take notes while they are responding and pay close attention to what they are saying.

Asking for advice is an excellent way to make a person feel important, however, it also has another huge benefit. The advice you get about your company, your products, or whatever you happen to be asking about, may give you an idea that could lead to some substantial new sales.

Some examples of what you can ask advise about: New products. Changes in your service. How to sell another buyer or customer. What they think of certain product features. How can you improve your service.

Try asking for a favor. We actually like someone more after doing something for them. If we do someone a favor we will have a positive feeling toward that person. In our attempt to get someone to think highly of US we tend to do things for them. What you want is for the customer or prospect to DO SOMETHING FOR YOU and they will actually like you more.

Customers will find a way to buy from you if they like you. They will also find a way NOT to buy from you if they don't like you.

The reason Thomas Edison sold all his inventions was simply this: Thomas Edison only invented things people would buy. To find out what people would buy he did extensive research and asked numerous experts their advice.

How many times have you come up with a seemingly brilliant idea, only to find out after investing time and money that it was all a waste of time. Perhaps the reason might be due to not seeking expert advice on the idea or project.

---------------------------

Comments:

---------------------------


There is nothing a person likes more than to be VALUED. Bob, you're right on target about asking for someone's Advice. When you ask for their advice, the internal chatter in a person mind stops and they will focus their attention on you. Advice accomplishes three different things. It shows you value them as a person; you have captured their attention (not always easy to do) and you put the client into a problem solving mode. One important point here is LISTENING, take NOTES and Don't Argue!!!! The next step is to slide seamlessly into the rest of your presentation.

What do YOU think??

**Teresa Cloninger**


I have a few computers at home and, as we all know, things happen to them when you get online or start playing around inside the programs. The man I take my PC to for repair at first was just fixing it and giving it back to me. One

33

time I asked what the problem was and he then offered to show me how to fix it myself. During subsequent trips to his shop he has shown me how to change parts in my PC which has saved me a ton of money. I think this is a good example of how asking for advice can be good for both parities.

**Brian Spraggins**


In general, people like to help others out. It's human nature. Traditional recruiting methods teach us that rather than leaving a message that says "I am looking for a Cost Accountant", rather say "You have been referred to me as an industry leader, could you help me with a project I am working on?" This usually appeals to their sense of ego (as does soliciting their advice) and also their sense of human spirit and wanting to help others out. It doesn't hurt when they feel comfortable giving you more information than you initially requested….possibly even a referral.

**Kristan Wilson**


"You are right on with your strategy to ask for advice. I used this strategy the other day on a new product line I carry and I was able to submit a proposal for $26,000 to a customer who had shut me down on that same topic a week before."

**Lewis Hoffman**

## 6. Why do people have a resistance to change?

You will almost always run into resistance when you ask someone to change. Their resistance comes from their unwillingness to let go of the status quo. People do not like to change. People resist even the best ideas.

A person resists an idea for a number of reasons. The resistance starts with a negative feeling about the product or idea. He or she has not looked into it yet. The immediate resistance is general.

First of all, there is a risk. What if the change does not pay off? Then he or she loses the cost and looks foolish. Something new means change and maybe the change will be uncomfortable. It might cause problems, and who needs problems? "I tried something like this before and it did not work out well, why take the risk?"

People in general do not want to hear about you or your idea or company. Even if you get them to listen, their generalized resistance adds strength to the objection.

However, you have to sell your ideas to get ahead. Your value to the customer cannot be known unless your products and services are tried. Be prepared for this resistance.

A lot of sales people ruin their credibility because they start to sell when the presentation is only half formed. They do not do their homework. The desire to get their idea sold is there, and it generates enough enthusiasm in them to propel them prematurely into the buyer's office and go for the close.

The buyer, motivated by his/her generalized resistance to anything new, looks for what is wrong. At this point, the buyer is NOT focusing on how to make it work. So the prospect raises some tough questions that you cannot answer. Not being prepared the sale dies.

By not being prepared you have lost more than the sale. You have lost some creditability. You have hurt your image. You have set the stage with a negative first impression.

From then on the buyer expects you to be unprepared. The buyer will look harder for holes in everything you present. And he or she figures that maybe it is a waste of time to talk with you. If they hear unsupported ideas, they will not be so willing to listen anymore.

This is the reason why many people fail at presenting their ideas. They are unprepared to overcome the resistance. They cannot handle the objections.

To overcome this resistance the best approach is to gather sufficient information about the buyer as well as the products or ideas you are going to present. Depending on what you are selling it may be necessary to make two or three information gathering calls before making the first presentation.

-------------------------------

Comments:

-------------------------------

You will do what I say, when I tell you to and LIKE it!!!! I hope this dose not sound too familiar! Why are so many companies hiring "change managers"; because it is Human nature to resist! How do you over come this? There are a couple of ways. One: slap them upside the head and tell them to just do it (not recommended by HR). Two: use research, trust and communication to gently pull the customer into the correct way of thinking. As a change manager (IE sales person) there is no magic bullet. IF you do the due diligence, ask the right questions, involve the right people (centers of influence) and COMMUNITCATE the benefits you are much more likely to close the sale (change the situation and status quo)! It is not rocket science- but it comes pretty close.

Stirred but not shaken,

**Teresa Cloninger**


No one likes to change, it's that simple. And it makes sense. Why leave what you're already accustomed to and what's comfortable to you to go to something you know little to nothing about. That's our jobs as sales people. We are to provide adequate information to a potential buyer to make them want to change and then make sure we help as much as possible to make it a smooth and comfortable transition.

**Matthew Thacker**


People stay in loveless marriages, dead end jobs and horrible living conditions, because of resistance to change. People fear the unknown and therefore are not willing to take the first steps to change their current situations. As sales people we are responsible for gently guiding our clients into a new and better situation. This usually requires negotiation, persistence and building trust from the sales

person. They have to buy you before they will buy from you.

**Kristan Wilson**

Bravo Kristan, you hit the nail on the head!

People DO tend to hold on to the familiar in a crisis situation, sometimes even when the "familiar same old-same old" is what created the crisis!

In today's changing environment things are tough. The economy, the weather, along with the competition from the big chains has cash flow in many independent businesses down significantly. It's not that the businesses themselves aren't operating profitably, there is just so much more pressure that when sales slow downt it creates an "uncomfortable" situation for the business. Many times the impulsive reaction is to cling even tighter to the old way of doing things when the customer should be looking for ways to improve operations and draw more business in or cut operating costs.

I have heard "We always did it this way and it's always worked fine" more times than I can count. Gasoline USED to be 29 cents a gallon. Employees USED to have a strong work ethic. The operators place of business USED to be one of 5 or 6 good dining establishments in town…before 20 chain restaurants opened in the same market and created a 20 more choices for people to eat out.

It is our responsibility as "partners" to show our customers HOW TO CHANGE.

**Chris Chase**


People get scared or annoyed with changes. Oftentimes it requires them to reach out of their comfort zone and do things differently. Not all people are open to that. In fact, most people aren't. This is a big challenge for salespeople trying to convince customers to switch services or products. It is the burden of the salesperson to adequately prove the benefit of changing and be prepared to do what it takes to help the customer make the change efficiently. The better a salesperson can communicate the benefit of the change they are asking the customer to make, the more likely the customer will buy.

**Marquesa Ortega**

## 7. How do you use the choice set up?

Nearly everyone in sales knows how to use the choice close; what day would you like delivery, Tuesday or Wednesday? What pack size would be best for you, 12 or 24? You ask the customer to choose between something you want and something else you want and them make the choice - you win both ways.

Now let's take it to a higher level by including the element of contrast. Give them a choice between something they don't want and something they didn't know they wanted until you presented the choice.

Let's say you are going to sell a house to a prospective buyer. The price you want is $100,000. You first take them to a $125,000 house that is overpriced by $25,000. Next you take them to a $75,000 house in need of $50,000 worth of repairs located in a poor area. NOW you take them to your perfectly priced house - $100,000. The choice for the buyer is clear.

How about the used car sales person? They first show you an old clunker that is overpriced and barely runs. Next they show you the care they really want to sell you. In your mind you are comparing the differences and thinking about what a great bargain!

43

You are talking to a computer sales person about purchasing a new system for your office. You tell the sales person all your requirements who is adding everything up on your list. The sales person now hits you with a whopping $10,000. As soon as you are over your shock you are presented with another choice - a package deal for only $3,000. What a deal! What an easy choice to make. Of course, that is what they wanted to sell you in the first place.

I am at the airport and the flight I am waiting to board is oversold. The attendant jokingly offers to pay $5,000 to anyone who is willing to give up their seat. He immediately admits that he was kidding and says he will pay $200 if anyone would be willing to give up their seat and take a later flight. No takers! Why? He misused the choice close set up. If he would have jokingly offered $25 and then raised it to $200 it would have seemed like a real deal.

Let's say you are going on a job interview and you are going to use the choice close set up. Arrange for two interviews, one immediately following the other. Have a friend go on the first appointment and have them intentionally screw up the interview. Then you go in, well prepared, on the second appointment for your interview and the choice becomes obvious.

If you think this sounds a little shady, consider this choice close set up used by undertakers. The undertaker will first show you a low budget, low price casket that is carefully positioned in a dark corner of the showroom. Then they show you the higher priced casket and point out all the benefits. Compared to the low end casket it is an easy choice to make. The closing statement is usually the one about the how the lower priced casket leaks and the higher priced doesn't! Works for me.

What does this have to do with you? The next time you present a product to a customer take two products instead of one. Take in an expensive, high end product along with the one you want to sell. Show them the over-priced high-end product first. After they get over their shock, bring out the one you wanted to sell in the first place and it will seem like and easy choice.

When I present my sales training program I always make the following comparison:

The American Management Association currently has a program available called Negotiating to Win. It is offered at 13 locations throughout the US at various times during the year. The cost; $1,675 per person with approximately 30% of the information covered being relevant to your business.

If you had 25 sales people it would cost you $41,875 plus the individual travel expenses for each sales person.

Makes my fee seem low, which it really is!

------------------------

Comments:

------------------------

Clear and Easy! Give them two choices, one you know is over priced and they would not consider and the one you need them to buy into to. This is a win-win situation for both.

As much as I hate to admit….this is so easy, my own teenagers know this strategy. "Mom here are the new Nike's for $165.00 that I just love, but if we cant get those, these that are ONLY $125.00 and I would wear also." HOOK, LINE, SINKER!!!!!

**Leslie Childers**


This section puts a lot in perspective from the "customers" view of your product. I think the choice set up is a great idea. I have never thought to use it on a customer, although I can clearly see how it is used all the time with things we purchase on a day-to-day basis. I believe giving people choices makes them feel powerful and that they are in control. First giving them the extreme option, followed by the option you really intend to sell makes a lot of sense. It seems to lure the customer in even more by showing them options that make the cost of what you are really trying to sell seem like a no brainer!!

**Brooke Knight**


This technique is used on everyone just about everyday. Especially at car dealerships. I remember it being used on me and I left with a car that I would have never purchased. The salesman first showed me an older Honda Accord that needed some work and told me that with my credit that is all I could afford, then all of a sudden the sales manager decides I can purchase the newer model Ford Mustang and bam it was done. Later I realized I hate Mustangs and had been taken for a ride.

**Kimberly Burgess**


I recently had a sampling with a customer at our location that prepares fresh cut steaks. I knew in advance that the customer was using a lower grade product. I sampled three steaks one Certified Angus, Choice and his current product. These selections were cuts with a much higher grade than what he was using. We prepared the product right in front of him to sample. He was surprised to find out the difference in taste and texture of the better product. We told him he could improve his menu item for just pennies more to the middle selection. He agreed.

**Roland DeGregorio**

## About the author Bob Oros

Regardless of whether you are reading one of his books or attending one of his programs, the most frequent comment is: "This guy has been there, he is one of us, I am going to use these strategies."

With over 2,000 speaking engagements in all 50 states and several international locations for manufacturers, distributors and associations, you can be sure you will get the results and information you are looking for. Prior to starting his speaking career, Bob served six years in the US Navy as a Communications Specialist and then worked his way from a street sales person to the position of National Sales Manager for a Fortune 200 company.

Bob has received awards for speaking, writing and marketing too numerous to mention.

# Contents of the entire course

Why Sales People Fail

-The Key to Selling Anybody

- The Power of Expectations

Add Value to Every Product

Never Make the First Offer

How to Justify Your Price

Lost in 60 Seconds

One Good Reason to Buy

Control a Buyer's Attitude

How to Create Demand

Smoke Screen Objections

Take the Risk Out of Sales

How Small Companies Get Big

www.ingramcontent.com/pod-product-compliance
Lightning Source LLC
Chambersburg PA
CBHW030011190526
45157CB00015B/2236